The Smart First-Time Home Buyer's Guide:

Avoid Making First-Time Home Buyer Mistakes

Updated: March 2019

Thomas. K. Lutz

Copyright © 2019 by T.K.Lutz
All Rights Reserved

Disclaimer:

No part of this publication may be reproduced or transmitted in any form or by any means, or transmitted electronically without direct written permission in writing from the author.

While all attempts have been made to verify the information provided in this publication, neither the author nor the publisher assumes any responsibility for errors, omissions, or misuse of the subject matter contained in this book.

This book is for entertainment purposes only, and the views expressed are those of the author alone, and should not be taken as expert instruction. The reader is responsible for their own actions.

Adherence to applicable laws and regulations, including international, federal, state, and local governing professional licensing business practices, advertising, and all other aspects of doing business in the U.S.A, Canada or any other jurisdiction is the sole responsibility of the purchaser or reader.

TABLE OF CONTENTS

Introduction 1
    Common Mistakes That Many
    Homebuyers make 3

Finding a Dream Home.. 13
    Consider your priorities 14
    Rent Or Buy – The Million-Dollar
    Question 19
    Location 24

Neighborhood Inspection 31
    Choosing the right neighborhood 31
    Undesirable locations 39
    Tips for neighborhood inspection 42
    Home requirements 45
    Making an offer 51
    Mortgage 52
    Inspection... 54

Appraiser 56
Closing price 57
Final Walk-through 58
Things Your Broker Won't Tell You.................... 60

Important home Buying tips...................................... 63

Conclusion 82

INTRODUCTION

Buying a home is a staggering life-changing decision. The experience of buying a home is intimidating and complex at best. So many things can run through your mind when you think about the perfect home you have always been dreaming of. It becomes even more nerve-wracking when the prospect of buying this perfect home looms above for you. There are limitless options and there is just about *everything* that you need to decide, re-consider and settle on. The sheer magnitude of the task of buying a home alone dampens your spirits and you begin doubting you could ever buy a home.

However, the admittedly unknown and often daunting territory of buying a home should not dissuade you from getting a home. If you want to avoid feeling too misplaced or weighed down during the entire process of buying a house, zero in on the two basic guiding principles of effective research and abiding thoroughness. Your buying choices must be backed up by an ample amount of research and you must not leave any corner unturned. You must be extremely, hair-splittingly thorough and diligent in the home buying process.

When you stumble across the phenomenon of buying a home, you will find that there will be a myriad of different challenges. Some will be very easy, like picking the right location and then there will be some, which will require professional help and advice, like managing funds and home-buying loans.

With the help of this detailed, in-depth tutorial, the entire buying process will become much easier. You will know exactly what to expect. Nothing makes something more difficult than not knowing what is in store for you. The element of surprise can take you down more than anything else. Some basic steps which are involved in the home buying process include choosing your preferred location, whether rural or urban, what kind of neighborhood are you looking for, is it a school district, proximity to work, or places to buy groceries, all of these are important factors to consider when choosing a location for your home.

Other factors include the kind of house that best suits your needs, and what is your budget, loan processes and details, finding a good and reliable agent, perusing through the various options outlined, settling on the perfect option, writing an offer and going through the escrow process, getting insurance, packing, shifting and finally, becoming a satisfied homeowner.

Common Mistakes That Many Homebuyers make

There are some obvious hurdles and mistakes that you must avoid when buying a home.

Mortgage Season; a Great Time to Buy a Home?

Often, homebuyers get overwhelmed during the low mortgages season. The housing market is not stagnant, they fluctuate – *a lot*. Due to many reasons, during the low mortgage season, it feels like it's the right time and you feel sure that this is the prime time to buy a home. However, you must not get swayed by the suitability of the time alone. There are many things that need to be kept in mind when buying a home, even if the time seems incredibly right. Just because the time is right, it does not mean it is the right time for *you*, especially if you will be moving soon. If the prospect of moving is in the near future, investing in a house will not be a good idea.

So Much to Buy – Such Little Money

Always remember that big money is involved when you are buying a house. Extra features, which seem rather extremely appealing, will involve a large amount of money and that added little facet of wooden windows will cost you *a lot*. When you are buying houses, you will feel inevitably scatterbrained and giddy. There are so many exciting new features, a delectable little patio, a backyard tucked in the corner, and a little balcony – it is extremely hard to say no to these. When buying a home, make sure you do not digress. You must know your limit and you should be prepared to seriously invest.

Eyes Too Big For Your Pockets

We have all heard of the phenomenon 'eyes too big for your pockets'; before you decide to be infatuated with a property, make sure you have your financial situation under control. Try not to look at properties which are beyond your budget; you will not only waste your time, you will also make your buying process increasingly difficult. You will never be able to settle on those that lie within your budget limits when you have your heart set on something which clearly exists within an entirely different realm.

Control Your Impulse

Impulsive and quick buyers should not let their all-too-eager and rash streak run the show for them. Instinct and sudden whim should take the back seat when you are buying a home. Home buying has a lot to do with your feeling towards the home which you really like, but it also has a lot more to do with the gritty details of the financial investment, budget, and credit.

Real Estate Agents: Dial Back on the Naiveté

First-time homebuyers often get so overwhelmed by the whole process of buying a house that they feel ever thankful to the real estate agents. However, it is very important to not be gullible and not fall into the several traps that the agents often line up for naïve homebuyers. It is very important to know where your agent's interest lies. If your agent has vested interests in the other party, you can rest assured that everything will not go as you have planned. This often happens in the case of dual agents.

The Constant Case of Free Advice

Take the advice of the agents when it comes to financial matters. However, take the advice with a pinch of salt. They are not professionals on your personal finance matters as no one is a better judge of whether this house is too expensive for you or not. No one can tell you that better than yourself. Remember that at the end of the day, they are looking for the commission and their target is a done deal. If you feel pressurized into signing something, do not do it.

Do Not Rush Into Anything

Always take your time. This cannot be stressed upon enough. Do not feel pressurized to buy anything or sign anything if your heart is not in it.

Handshakes: No Honor Code Applies Here

There is no integrity in a handshake. Do not fall for the handshake deal. This is not a done deal. Whenever you have to finalize something, get it in writing. You are most likely to go home and celebrate after a handshake deal only to find out the next day that someone outbid you and your cozy little handshake moment disappeared into thin air. Never trust a verbal agreement; it is of little to no significance. In business, verbal agreements mean next to nothing. Even if you try to challenge someone in court, you will realize you have no legal standing. Verbal agreements, gestures, and handshakes are not binding.

Payment Shock

All home buyers need to understand and effectively deal with a commonly occurring condition 'payment shock'. Numbers sound just fine when they have spoken aloud, they seem quite all right even in fine print, we shake on it, we sign the documents and we go home. When the time of the payment arrives, customers suffer from payment shock. Nothing seems more palpable and real than actual, real-time money being transferred over to someone else. Nothing seems more solid than this and this payment shock must be dealt with beforehand.

Home Inspection

Several new homebuyers skip the home inspection. This is extremely vital. Most of the time, the buyers are looking to cut down on the cost. What they do not realize is that if you do not hire professionals to scan and inspect the house for cheap, low-cost construction material, faults in the mechanical rooms, drains, and pipes, you will end up spending way more in the future. You will soon find yourself fixing problems that you did not see fit to fix before you decided to purchase the property. Home inspectors flag faulty construction material, check and inspect attics and basements. Results compiled by the home inspectors also give you a good insight into how to maintain your house you are planning on buying.

Save the Emotions for the Negotiation

It is very important for homebuyers to keep their emotions in check when buying a house or perusing through options. It is advised to not act overtly in-love with the house as this will obviously play up against you when you are trying to bargain and strike a fair deal with the seller or the seller's agent. You should also not get too fixated on the small problems and complain too much as this will also lead to the broker or agent checking you off the list of the probable buyers. It is smart to play up the small problems to your own benefit and bring them up while negotiating.

Brand-New-Everything Syndrome

Sometimes homebuyers, after buying a new home, start living in a shiny new bubble of 'newness'. Just because you have bought a new home, this does not mean that you start eyeing the ratty old lounge furniture and immediately replace it with new ones because it seems better and more suited to the beautiful new home. Homebuyers often drown in debt, right after a huge purchase of buying a house. Once you have bought a new house, take a breather, calm down and let your finances recover from a massive blow. Not everything in the house needs to be replaced to match the new house.

Pay Some Attention to Your Credit Report

It is very important to get your credit report free of any past blemishes and bad-record stains.

Before you dive deep into home buying research and begin comparing one house to the other, shift your attention to more pressing matters, like your credit score and your credit report. Before you can even set foot in a house, you will be required to present the real estate agent with a copy of your hopefully clean and pristine credit card report. You must get your priorities in order before you start perusing through housing options.

Be Realistic

More than anything else, this is what causes most problems. Homebuyers often forget that not everything will be exactly as they pictured. Your wish list might have a plethora of things, all neatly sorted together, which you would like to see in your brand new house but it is advisable to remain prepared for a reality check; not every single thing will be the way you always dreamed of. Prepare to let go and prepare to accept before you decide to start looking at houses. You must not be so close-minded when you are preparing to buy a house.

Other rookie mistakes that homebuyers often make include not setting out enough time to research the neighborhood that their new dream home is located in. it is not just the house that you are concerned with, it is also the vicinity and the locality and it is as important as the paint color of the wall of your bedroom. In addition to this, homebuyers often pay too much attention to things that they 'want'. It is important to focus on things you need and not get swept too far into obscurity by focusing on things you just want.

Considering and keeping in mind the resale value of your home is also very important and many homebuyers often conveniently skip this part, especially if they find themselves to be too 'in love' with a particular home. No one can predict the future so it is always good to be secure.

Buying a home is a life-changing decision. It is a weighty and a massive verdict so it must be made with utmost care and precision. It is better to know beforehand what to expect and how to avoid commonly occurring mistakes, as opposed to diving in unprepared.

Finding a Dream Home

Nearly everyone, at some point in his or her life, stumbles across the much-visited alley of 'finding a dream home'. Everyone has his or her own idea of a perfect home; the flawless windows, the picture-perfect view, and the seamless little road leading up to the impeccable humble *or* not-so-humble abode.

We romanticize and fantasize about virtually the whole house, which we have been dreaming about all our lives, carefully conjuring up the idealistic fine points such as the particulars of the floors and the ceilings.

We, quite literally, break it down to every little detail – all rolled into a delectable little slice of real estate perfection.

Consider your priorities

Finding a perfect home becomes more than just being a desire, it crops up as everyone's top priority, at least at some point in his or her life. Buying a perfect home is nothing short of an achievement. Everybody has a different idea regarding the ideal home; once you buy a home, you want it to fit you and your family snugly like a glove – it has to be built just *right,* just for *you.*

The undeniable and the inevitable add-on of the emotional-element makes the purchase and the hunt for a home even more challenging and complicated out of all real estate purchases. If you are fortunate enough, you might get multiple chances to buy new homes. However, for most people, this is "once-in-a-lifetime" real estate purchase endeavor. The emotions peak, the budget is often constricted, and the dreams and the hopes regarding the future home skyrocket, this is all coupled with the inescapable wish to remain satisfied with the purchase in the long-standing future too.

The Inevitable Butterflies and the Jitters

It is quite an exciting and even a slightly unsettling position to be in – when you are looking to buy your own home. There are so many options to choose from and just about anything and everything matters and is quite close to your heart.

You set out, looking for the perfect home, with one determination in mind: *It has to be perfect. And this where we come in because we have got your needs fully covered!*

Some important tips, which you must keep in mind when you are beginning the hunt for your house, include budget, size, style, location, rent/buy, and family. It may sound fairly easy and you might just try to tackle every aspect with a surefire response, however, it is not that simple. Everything comes, hand in hand, with mind-numbing intricacies and details and, before you know it, you will find yourself tripping on the niceties.

Therefore, it is very important to go into the house-hunt with a clear mind, knowing what to expect and how to deal with important issues first. The first and the foremost consideration, while looking for a perfect home, is budget – no questions asked.

Budget

This is the least fun dynamic of the entire home buying process and, therefore, we try to shove it back down to the depths, covering it up with more exciting details, like, choosing between the fancier wooden floors and the more deluxe interior design. It is a lot more stimulating to flit around between modernizations, upgrades, interiors, and aesthetics and color combinations.

However, the budget concern rears its calculative little head up soon enough once you have figured out all the dolled-up details of the house and the more delayed the budget issue gets, the more rapidly all your hopes and dreams get dashed to nothing. You have to get the numbers right before you build your dream home on a pile of virtual dreams. Some of the important costs that you have to consider while deciding upon budget limitations and concerns, include the rent rates, mortgage rates, and cost of living in a particular area or location.

Do Not Over-Estimate

A good rule of thumb, when estimating the affordability of your perfect home, bases calculations on your *lowest* annual income. Do not stretch your budget to the farthest limits to fit your lofty ideals and wishes of a home. You must remember that aside from the monthly mortgage payments, there will also be other costs, including monthly utility costs, local taxes, and other society fees, associated with the area that you are living in.

Getting Down to Business

When you find your most preferred home, and decide to make an offer on any given property, which fits all your requirements and seems good enough, get in touch with the seller directly or through a reliable agent and get right down to business. This means that you should get down to the sand and grit of the financial aspects to get things into perspective before you finalize anything at all.

Do the Math

You need to get an accurate and exact breakdown of the monthly and yearly payments. Some monthly payments sound 'just about right'. However, once you calculate them on an annual basis, you often realize the true impact of the entire lump sum, which may seem affordable, when divided over a period of months.

You also need to keep in mind that your income will not rise dramatically in the future; the most dependable jobs, too, face the dangers of impending retirement, layoffs or any ill-starred incident and all these possibilities need to be accounted for and kept in mind when deciding upon a home. When buying a home, there are several options, which can be considered to suit your particular budgetary situation; you must choose that one house, which allows you to have breathing space at the end of every month, budget-wise.

Rent Or Buy – The Million-Dollar Question

Other options include renting out a house, instead of buying it outright. Buying a home is not always the answer – this is extremely essential to fathom. There are several situations in which buying a house will not be ideal, especially if you might be moving soon in the near future, or you are just out of college and feeling good about yourself and have some misguided ideas about busting your entire budget on buying a house that you may or may not need forever after all. It is always a good idea to compare mortgage rates with rent rates and choose the one which suits you the most.

Sometimes renting might just make more sense, so prepare yourself to not get thrown off by the idea. Until and unless you plan to live in a house for at least a period of ten years or more, do not buy it; rent it out instead. This is important because it takes at least a period of ten years for you to break even; real estate property prices, especially when it comes to residential houses, rise about 3% to 4% every year. After at least a decade has passed and a subsequent increase in price and value of the house has occurred, only then you will be able to counterbalance the fees and the commissions, which you bore the brunt of, during the purchase of the house.

Rationalize - Do Not Speculate

However, financially speaking, if you consider waiting too long to see when the prices will fall, you will be doing yourself a disservice.

Often people are so caught up trying to wait for the low mortgage season to swing by that they forget that they will eventually be paying off the difference in the form of high-interest rates anyway, so it really is just wasting time. It would make sense to wait around for the prices of something like *gold* to plummet because that is something we just *desire*, we do not really need it, so it would be okay to wait. Speculators would do that and that would make sense but equating speculation about a luxury as unnecessary as gold to a necessity as indispensable as homeownership is quite irrational. We must realize that nobody *needs* gold, whereas, everyone *needs* a place to live. Therefore, different rules apply. If you find a perfect home and the numbers add up, do not wait around for the mortgage rates to fall.

Home Style

The home-style that you choose must be consistent with your personality; it should be the kind of home that you would feel satisfied with day-in and day-out. Your home is not a pit stop; it the place where you will come back at the end of every day and it should be ideal and perfect according to all aspects and nobody is a better judge of that than you are.

Personality Type

Homestyle refers to the style of living of the general, overall aesthetic of the home or the property. The way your home looks, the outer and the interior appearance is what makes 90% of the home; it is very important. If you have an outward, unrestricted personality, you would be better suited to a single home, which you can customize according to your specific needs and wants.

Condominium Style Living

Condominium style living is preferable for those who want a fine balance between single home living style, in addition to hotel-style facilities; in condo-style living, you will get the best of both worlds. Other home styles include community-style living, gated-communities, and town living.

The outward appearance, the construction, and the architecture design of every home will differ based on where it is located, whether it is in a community, a town, or in a condominiums building. A modern, single-block condominium will differ greatly from a Victorian lodge.

Home Size

It is very important to come to terms with rationalizing when you are deciding on the size of your house. Be realistic about how much space you really need. The number of people who will be living in a house and whether even a single person needs all that space can easily deduce the answer to the home size question. Whichever home style you choose, you must keep the size in mind too. If you buy a house, which is too small for your family, you will spend the rest of your life, constantly trying to make space for yourself and your family.

Space Considerations – Extremely Vital

You need to understand how much space you will require and how much space your family members will need. A wise decision at the start will prevent relocating problems in the future. As it goes, it is quite irrational to buy a large, sprawling house if you have a small family or a single person. You will only be tying up your money in useless concrete that you will probably never even use. Along with a lot of unused space, you will also be adding unnecessary maintenance costs to your budget. It is a good idea to compare the current space you are living in- are all your family members comfortable or do they have to share rooms to make space for each other? Current size is a good estimate of your needs.

Future Family Extensions Must Be Remembered

Newly married couples need to keep in mind the aspect of extending their family in the future so the additional space factor will be important to remember when deciding on the size of the house. Preferably, you should reach a happy medium – you do not need to get caught up in too much space or get bogged down by too little.

Location

Your House Comes with Strings Attached

Always remember that your house does not exist in isolation. It will be surrounded by others and you need to decide whether it is suitable for you or not. Your house will exist along with other houses, forming a larger community. If you are the sort who enjoys peace and quiet, do not expect that kind of serenity from a bustling commercial housing zone. You need to decide what some of your needs are and whether these needs coincide with the location of the house that you have in mind.

Do Not Get Blinded

When looking at houses, we are often blinded by the sheer number of things that need to be considered, that we tend to forget the importance of the location. We begin looking at the house as a single entity and often exclude the reality of the surrounding location and the neighborhood. The house is only the tip of the iceberg; a great, big beautiful house is nothing if it exists in a run-down locality.

Neighborhood Considerations

What kind of neighbors do you have? Are you willing to put up neighborly noise? Are you okay with the idea of a long morning walk to the bus station? Are you used to running down to the nearest coffee shop to grab a cup of early morning

Joe? Do you have all these facilities in the house that you are considering?

Drive Around and See For Yourself

Do not take somebody else's word for this. These important questions need to be dealt with by you, and you alone. It is a good idea to test out the house and the locality that you are considering. Drive around and note the time it takes you to get to places like the bus station, the malls, the local grocery store, and the coffee shops. You need to see what the local nearby parks are like, and what exists at the end of the shiny new road that your house is built on. When considering the location of the house, it is advisable to take an in-depth tour of the nearby area, either by walking or driving around. Check out the local restaurants and see if you can visualize yourself living there easily or not.

Reminder: You Are Not Living In a Bubble

The location often gets pushed far back as an af-terthought. Do not let this happen to you. Try not to see your house as an exclusive single piece of property. Remember when you are paying for the house, you are also paying a significant amount for the neighborhood and the location as well so it must be up to your standards. You must realize that this is something that you can do literally nothing about; if a house exists in a certain location, you cannot get up and demolish the entire area to suit your needs. You can break down and rebuild houses from scratch but locations? Not likely.

Do not be Afraid to Walk Away; There Will be others

When buying your perfect home, do not settle for anything less than what you have dreamed of, especially when it comes to location. If anything at all feels like a compromise, do not force yourself to do it.

Family

After everything has been seen, said and done, do not forget your family. It is very important to consider who you are going to be living with. Do not spearhead the house purchasing on your own, giving no regard to other people's wishes and dreams. After all, a home's true worth comes from a loving family living together.

Family Discussion is The Key

Take into consideration what the others have to say about the house and what are they looking for. Not everyone views things from your perspective; so find a happy medium and a fine balance. Think about all the things that you wish to do in your home in the coming years. If you like to host parties then carefully consider the layout of the house. It should be spacious and comfortable enough to welcome your guests easily. .

Think about the activities of all the family members- are your children the sorts who lean towards sports or just basic recreational activities? Give a consideration to the outdoor space in addition to the interior of the house, like for example, finding a house with a backyard, a swimming pool or a ground big enough to install nets, swings and enough room to play in.

Personal Space

Realize what kind of family you have; do all the family members require their own personal space? If yes, look for a house with plenty of room so everyone can get their own private space without interfering or cause too much trouble for anyone else. When buying a house, you have to keep everyone happy and that is the exact definition of a perfect home.

Put Your Heart and Soul in It

When all considerations and all factors have been decided upon and all the numbers and the budget concerns add up and make sense, it is time to take the plunge. Understand that no matter how perfect the house might be, it will always need a fair amount of customization according to your very own specific needs.

This is where you need to put your heart in the house to make it your perfect home.

Even the most perfect dream house is going to need a little bit of tweaking around here and there to make it resonate with the essence of you and your family. Even if you find all the features that you ever wanted in a house, from your eyes, there will always be room for improvement so make room for that in your mind, when settling upon a house. You will get a perfect 99%, at best, and to bring it up to a perfect 100%, you have to alter it according to your own needs and specifications.

Everyone deserves to find their perfect dream home and it is very much possible with the right kind of guidance and research backing up the entire process. By using these vital factors and guidelines, you can easily buy your perfect home, without stumbling across any hitches. These factors will help you to concentrate on the important elements and, most importantly, these elements will help you to prioritize in the right way. There is no reason that you should wait for your dream to turn into reality.

NEIGHBORHOOD INSPECTION

Choosing the right neighborhood

Choosing a home is much more than just choosing the building layout and structure. It is going to be a major part of your lifestyle and a major investment. So choosing the right neighborhood is a must. Location is critical to determining the aspects of your daily life, in and around your new home.

Geography

The geographical area in which you buy your home will have a major impact on your lifestyle. The climate, the economy, the laws of the state will all have to be looked at closely and carefully to buy a home in a particular neighborhood and state that is right for you. For instance, buying a home in California will mean lots of sunshine and a neighborhood in Nevada might mean future drought and a drop in real estate prices. Buying a home in Florida as compared to Colorado will again constitute different lifestyle choices.

Urban vs. Peri-Urban vs. Rural

Do you want to live in an urban neighborhood? Of course, there will be a lot of positives associated with living in the city, like less travel time and good leisure and schooling opportunities. As opposed to that, the negatives of an urban neighborhood will surely be the high crime rates, high levels of pollution and more noise.

Rural neighborhoods will give you freedom of space, as opposed to the congestion of urban living. Rural areas will also have relatively more peace and quiet. However, such areas might lack a lot of facilities you take for granted in urban living.

Peri-urban neighborhoods in the suburbs give you the best of both worlds. You can experience the peace and quiet of rural areas and have access to most of the facilities that modern living requires, with the city usually just a train ride away.

Safety

Safety plays a key role when determining which area to live in. If your neighborhood isn't safe, then is it really worth living in? You might pay less in order to live in an area where the crime rate is high, but more often than not, you will end up paying much more for the crime against you.

Safety and security rank higher for people with families than single people, so the choice of the neighborhood might vary according to marital and family status. Another major downside to high crime neighborhoods is the low resale value of the housing. So choose wisely when moving into a neighborhood that is unsafe.

School Districts

Education has always been the cornerstone of society and with increased competition, it has become critical to a child's success. Choosing neighborhoods with good schools is imperative for parents who have high aspirations for their kids. Paying that extra few dollars might be worth it in the end if that means better schooling opportunities.

Remember that nothing is greater or more important than your child's future.

Recreation and Nature

Parks and recreation are vital to your leisure activities. Living in a neighborhood with close proximity to these can be a major plus point. You could then engage in outdoor activities and spend quality time with your family. Places near scenic beauty tend to cost more, but also hold immense value. A home on the side of a lake or near the beach all have their perks.

View

The view from the house itself should be appealing. A neighborhood that does not have scenic beauty will tend to sell at lower prices. A view does not necessarily have to be a natural beauty- it can very well be a panoramic view of the city. Imagine living in a neighborhood from where you can see the city lights in their full glory. A neighborhood that has great views of the mountains or lakes will be equally pleasing. Aesthetics are a key factor to consider when selecting a neighborhood. A property with a nice view always has an advantage when it comes to reselling.

Entertainment/ Leisure activities

Entertainment and leisure activities are crucial determinants of modern-day life. Without them, life would surely be incomplete. A neighborhood that has access to a multitude of restaurants will be a major positive. Neighborhoods that are close to malls, cinemas and other entertainment venues tend to provide a better quality of living. However, these localities cost more money so many people choose to drive to these places rather than live close by and just walk to them. But for those who can afford it, living close to high-end shops and boutiques is highly desirable.

Conformity

Does the neighborhood conform to the standards of your house? Most people want to live in areas that have houses that are roughly as old as their own home. They also want to live around people who generally share similar beliefs. Most often than not, people want to live around other people who have similar interests and thoughts. For example, a liberal family might find it hard to live in a predominantly conservative neighborhood.

Apart from people in the neighborhood, similar properties in terms of age value and size are also desirable. No one wants to live in a mansion next to small houses or in an apartment building in situated close to a slum.

Economic stability

You should definitely consider a neighborhood that is economically stable. These neighborhoods have seen the booms come and go and survived the bust. These neighborhoods have proven their value over the years and stood the test of time.

These sort of localities tend to be good investments for the future. These neighborhoods have withstood the artificial price hikes and they have shown consistently that they are worth the money invested in them. Therefore, it is a wise move to buy a house in such places.

Public Transport

These days a lot of traveling is required for one reason or another. Activities like schooling, entertainment and most importantly work mean that you get to travel a lot during the day. Hence, a good neighborhood must have easy access to public transport.

Often, one public transport source is not enough. Desirable places to live mostly have multiple links to public transports like bus stops, railway tracks, subways, sky-trains, mass rapid transits, and highways.

When selecting a neighborhood, you might want to look for links to major public transport facilities, but remember, there are downside living way too close to public transportation as well, because of the noise level.

Health services

A good place to live must have easy access to decent healthcare facilities. Your neighborhood must have a basic health unit with easy access to public hospitals. If you select a neighborhood that is far away from decent healthcare, you are not only risking your life, but the lives of your loved ones as well.

It could cost you extra bucks, but that will be a price worth paying when faced with a medical emergency in which every second might be critically important to save a life. The least that you can look for in a neighborhood is whether it falls under the coverage of an air ambulance service. A service such as this would help mitigate major disasters from taking place.

Jobs

The time you spend on your commute to work directly affects your disposable income, your work quality and the time you have left for the family. Living close to the place you work can do wonders for your work and personal life balance.

Whilst looking at houses, look for a neighborhood close to where you're working so that you can enjoy a higher quality of life.

Proximity to friends and family

The ideal house only becomes a home when you have your friends and family to share it with. So be sure to look for a neighborhood that is close to where most of your friends and family reside. This way, you will have the added benefit of an active and engaging social life in your new home.

Undesirable locations

The following is a list of locations in which you should avoid buying a house. These locations not only reduce the resale value of your house, they also tend to decrease your quality of life. These locations tend to take a lot out of you so try and avoid the following places and the perils of living close to them.

- Places with Commercial or industrial land close by will tend to be highly polluted. Pollution is detrimental to your health and reduces the peace of mind you get from your house. You cannot control the people who litter in front of your abode. You will also have to deal with loud noises during the day that constitute commercial and industrial activity. Both these areas will interfere with the peace and quiet that you seek. Air pollution next to factories is harmful to health. It is thus advisable to stay away from neighborhoods which have the above-listed factors in abundance.

- Neighborhoods near the highway, railroad, and airport platforms are going to cause you a lot of inconveniences. The amount of noise pollution that you will have to deal with is staggering. Air pollution will also be a major factor as they will all utilize vehicles functioning on fossil fuels. It would be a wise move to stay away from these neighborhoods.

- Crime ridden areas are to be avoided at all costs. No amount of savings resulting from buying a home in crime-ridden areas is worth it. Such a place might end up hurting you. Try and avoid areas that have historically high crime rates. A home is where you and your children feel safe. Do not destroy that peace of mind by living in a crime-infested area.

- Economically deprived localities tend to have those people who take zero care of their houses. Such neighborhoods boast of junk cars on every street corner and high gang violence. These areas should be avoided at all costs.

- Natural hazard-prone areas can prove disastrous. Some people often take the risk, thinking that the chance of a natural disaster hitting is small. When a natural disaster does hit, the effects are usually catastrophic, so it is not worth taking a chance. Moreover, try your best to avoid hurricane and earthquake-prone zones. Do not live close to large forest areas where forest fires could easily start. It is also safe to avoid living in snowy mountains where avalanches might be common.

Tips for neighborhood inspection

The following list highlights some inspection tips that you might want to take into account before selecting an area to live in. These will help you get a better understanding of the area and prevent you from incurring fraud.

Potential neighbors

Always research and ask around in the neighborhood to get an idea of what kind of people will be living next door. The type of community you move into will determine a lot of your household activities.

Visit the neighborhood during the day and night

This is an important step in order to get a true feeling of the neighborhood. Some neighborhoods feel very safe and welcoming during the day, but have a disconcerting silence during the night. Be sure to sleep on your decision before moving in. Do not judge a neighborhood on how it looks during weather extremes. The best judge is in everyday weather conditions. Moreover, lighting and security at night should be given special consideration.

Look at the statistics

Try and collect as much neighborhood statistics as possible. They will be your guide into the past of the neighborhood on which basis you can determine whether the place will be safe for you and your family in the future.

Price

Look at the price registry databases to get a true estimate of the house. The asking price is negotiable and selling records of similar nearby houses will give you the best idea of what to pay.

Gut feeling

This might sound very simple, but listen to your gut feeling. If a neighborhood doesn't feel right, it is better not to buy a house there. In the end, your peace of mind matters much more than anything else.

Local authorities

The efficiency of the local authorities should be checked beforehand. Look at the schedules of garbage collection and other utilities.

The condition of other houses

Looking at the condition of other houses is a quick and easy tip to understanding the true value of the neighborhood. The condition of the other houses reflects on the class of people that lives there as a whole.

House Inspection

Home requirements

After selecting the perfect neighborhood, you need to search for a home that best suits you. The house of your dreams is what you define it to be. Hence, be mindful of picking a house that can best fulfill your current as well as potential needs.

New or Old

Do you require a house that is new or one that is used? A used house may cost you less money but it will have its own problems. A new house can have newer design features that accommodate more features in an efficient manner, but could, however, end up costing more.

Historic or Modern

Do you require a house that is modern, tech-savvy or are you one of the traditionalists who prefer the old school look with a touch of history?

Be sure to state your requirements clearly to the agent when looking for a house.

Bedrooms

Be sure to look for bedrooms not only according to your current needs, but future needs as well. If you plan to expand your family, look for one extra bedroom at least. The size and type of house will also determine the number of bedrooms you can have. A townhouse, condo or apartment all have a differing number of bedroom options.

Bathrooms

Bathroom needs can vary according to your requirements. Having only one bathroom for multiple users will end up with a long wait in the morning. A family should thus preferably look for a house with more than one bathroom.

Kitchen Design

The kitchen designs these days are available in an amazing variety. You can have anything from traditional American kitchens to having kitchens inspired by Japanese and European designs.

Floor

Wooden flooring or marble floors with synthetic tiling are all available at your request. Be sure to choose the house that has the type you desire.

Interior Design

Architects have come up with very creative designs for household interiors. The special thought is now given to everything from lighting to the colors and space requirements. All of these are governed by how the interior is set, so be sure to look carefully at the interior to judge which house gives you the best possible options.

Pet requirements

If you have a pet, check whether your house is pet-friendly. Check whether it has the small pet doors if it has a garden for them to play in and if it has any objects or fixtures that could pose a threat to your pets.

Inspecting all these elements will lead you to select the ideal abode. The house of your dreams will not just appear out of the blue. You will have to be mindful of all these minor details and select the house according to your needs.

Home inspection

A home inspection is basically making sure that the property is safe and inhabitable. This also gives an estimate of what the property is worth and what condition it is in.

Inspection standards

There are a few major kinds of inspections carried out, such as:

- Structural inspection: the walls, foundation, paint, drainage, and roof are all checked. Major and notable holes and cracks are searched for. This inspection will determine the general structural integrity of the house.

- Mechanical inspection: this includes checking for working toilets, heating, cooling, plumbing, and electronics.

- Miscellaneous inspection: this inspection is carried out to look beyond the structural and mechanical issues. This inspection includes rodent or pest problems in addition to the proper working of doors etc.

- Required repairs: Required repairs may be anything from defective paint to standing water. Make sure you get these issues resolved before moving in.

Getting the right inspector

You should always look for the best inspector who carries out the best inspection. He or she should:

- Belong to a professional inspecting company

- Have carried out more than **a 1000 inspections**

- give you detailed written reports
- adhere to standard practices
- Have proper training
- Have a good reputation in the market

Home inspection mistakes

Common home inspection mistakes include;

- Not inspecting a new house- whether new or old, inspections are mandatory.
- Choosing a cheap inspector: this will not save you money. Rather, it will you in the future.
- Not being present when the inspection takes place and missing out on important information.
- Not listening to the recommendations of the inspector: this is a major mistake as not listing to experts might cause you big bucks, especially when it comes to

resolving major repairs or other problems you should have resolved timely.

- Expecting too much out of home inspectors: home inspectors are not supermen. They are bound to make mistakes. Always leave a margin for human error.

Buying a House checklist

Making an offer

- Be smart when bidding for a house. You do not want to overpay or be made to look like a fool. Ask around for the prices of similar houses that have been sold recently in the neighborhood. Be sure to conduct a detailed comparative price analysis so you don't end up overpaying.

- Demand clearly what you want and don't want in a house. The furniture and fixtures that you want to be part of the deal should be stated upfront. The color of the drapes and walls should also be revealed clearly. Be sure to make your preferences known.

- Stress on the closing date in negotiations according to your own advantage. If you are not in a dire hurry to move-in, try and delay the time so that you can get the maximum work done and concessions from the sellers as possible. The more you delay, the more you will put the sellers on a back foot, but don't delay for too long as that might hurt the deal.

- Buy a home with a home warranty. This is necessary as a home warranty gives you protection from damages and free repairs for up to a year after your purchase of the house. In the negotiation, try and have the seller buy a house warranty so that you could benefit from it later on.

Mortgage

- When getting a house mortgage, try and ask for referrals from the people you know. These might include friends, family or your real estate agent. All of these referrals could help you get to people who will offer you loans at low interest. If you qualify for membership to local credit unions, they will also help you get lower interest rates.

- Calculate down payment so that you can save yourself extra costs. If you pay at least 20% of the principle, this will save you from private mortgage insurance. Be sure to save costs from all the places where possible.

- Quotes from Multiple lenders. Be sure to take quotes from multiple lenders to get the best interest rate out there. Consult multiple lenders to get an idea of the market rate. Consult mortgage brokers as well as bankers to get the best possible deal.

- Decide on whether to pay upfront to lower interest rates or prolong your interest payments. If you have the capital available, it is best to pay off as much principle as possible in one go. The lower the remaining amount, the lower the interest you will end up paying for it.

Inspection

- Qualified inspector: a qualified inspector is an investment. Paying a bit more for a qualified inspector will end up saving a lot on later repairs. Always look for the best inspectors that have at least 1000 inspections under their belt. Look for one that is accredited and has a good reputation in the market. Do remember that quality doesn't come cheap.

- Detailed report: a detailed report is a must for inspection. Ask for one beforehand with all the details and photographic evidence. Be sure to know any and everything that is wrong in advance. Request a detailed inspection report beforehand.

- Additional assessment: sometimes there are houses that are built a bit differently than the standard houses. For these houses, it is better to ask for additional inspections. Consult your real estate broker and have the things that seem ambiguous checked out in-depth.

- Be present at the inspection: your presence at the inspection is vital. Though you are no expert and can't figure out the technical aspects, you must be present. You can learn a lot about the house at that moment. Be sure to keep asking questions about the structure and layout of the house. During the inspection, you are sure to learn about the electrical circuits, the gas pipelines, and the water system.

- Take written estimates from the repairman: these estimates will help you with the house price. Your agent could then give these estimates to the house sellers and ask them to have them fixed or have then deducted from the house price. These estimates of repairs will save you quite a lot of bucks.

- Price credit: there is an alternative to having the seller schedule the repairs. You can ask the seller to reduce the repairs price of the house and conduct the repairs yourself at a later time. This is feasible for those of you who are handy with housework and cannot afford to delay the purchase.

Appraiser

- Have an appraiser appraise the house: to get a true judgment of the house's value, you should conduct this practice. The appraiser will give you a market estimate, according to what is agreed in the contract. Make sure to make him aware of what is being sold and what isn't. Your money-lender will hire the appraiser so that they can understand the worth of the asset they are lending money against.

- Ask for a list of comparable houses: this will help you get a better understanding of where your home stands in comparison to other similar houses that have been recently appraised. You will get to judge the improvements to your house as compared to them and identify areas your house is lacking.

- Look around for title insurance: title insurance protects you against legal damages to your property. Try and look at the best rates available. You do not have to buy it from the first company that offers it. The coverage difference isn't that much in title insurance, so look for the cheapest option. It will provide almost the same coverage as the more expensive options.

Closing price

- Consult an attorney: you should make sure you are not getting fooled. Hire an attorney and have him go through the contract. There are often details in the fine print that might come back to hurt you.

- Set your interest rate: have your interest rates locked in a month or so before the purchase so that you are safe from any fluctuations. It is better to consult a financial analyst if possible.

- Obtain detailed closing costs: transfer taxes or other expenses might surprise you later on. Be sure to have the details of all the costs involved.

- Be mindful of bogus fees: if you are being charged for mundane services or services that are free, have they removed from the bill. After all, you don't want to over-pay.

Final Walk-through

- Verify all appliances: be sure that all appliances, electrical and non-electrical are in working condition.

- Verify all taps and toilets: you do not want faulty plumbing to ruin your perfect home.

- Verify all electrical outlets: you should check whether the wiring is all correct and all the sockets are functional and safe.

- Verify the air conditioning and heating system: fixing these, later on, can be a real big problem. Be sure to have them checked and rechecked.

- Check for water damage: any seepage or moisture damage will cause greater harm in the future to your house. Check for that carefully.

- Check for termite/vermin: these can be a major pain and cause a lot of damage to wooden houses. Be sure that your house is termite and vermin free. Always look in the basement and the attic for these creatures.

- If anything is found damaged, be sure to negotiate closing credit before closing a deal. You don't want to pay for damaged good, do you?

Things Your Broker Won't Tell You

- Negotiable fees: the brokers tend to hide the fact that the fees they charge can be negotiated and the house prices are negotiable as well.

- Inspection details that could kill a deal are often hidden by the brokers. Do not trust the brokers and always carry an independent inspection of the facility.

- They add contract clauses without legal counsel just to confuse you and try and save themselves from possible contingencies. Having an attorney go through the contract is a good option.

- You may not need the broker to make a deal after all. They charge commissions and will make you feel that they got you the best possible deal, but you can directly communicate yourself with the selling party online.

- Some houses are kept secret by the brokers for themselves or their special clients. These houses are not advertised to the general public so that the brokers can make underhand profits out of them.

- The house price is hiked often enough by the brokers. Try and look at comparable prices of similar property sold nearby to get the best price estimate.

- That you could do better with another agent is a secret no broker will tell you. After all, there are brokers with different competency levels so do look around.

- That they don't have complete knowledge is a fact no broker would want to admit. Sometimes the brokers just turn to old selling techniques and cliché sales pitches.

- Some brokers won't tell you how desperate they are. Overeager brokers should be avoided. You shouldn't feel any pressure and make a decision in your own time and by considering all the facts.

IMPORTANT HOME BUYING TIPS

Buying a home is one of the biggest investments you can make. Therefore, it should be done in a strategic and informed manner so as to minimize the risks. This chapter is full of useful tips that will make your purchasing decision easier and help you make an educated and informed purchase.

Looking at budget (own or rent)

What you can afford:

Can you afford to buy a house? Are you better off renting a property?

These questions should be at the top of your list when thinking about moving into a new place. Remember to consult with real estate experts as well as financial analysts. You would not want to buy just before a possible bust in housing prices or at the peak of a boom.

Also, if you are not sure that you can stay in the house for at least the medium run then buying a property is not the right idea. It is much better to rent. If you really want to buy the house then carefully evaluate your future plans, keeping in mind both your family and career.

The next thing to consider is whether you have the finances to pay off the mortgage cost. Also, can you handle all the additional costs associated with purchasing a house?

Make sure to make some financial considerations before purchasing a house. The following tips are very useful;

Evaluate your credit history and pay off any outstanding debt. This will get you much better terms for a mortgage loan.

- Aim for a house you can easily afford by looking at your sources of income.

- Get professional financial help. Although you will find a lot of cost calculators on the internet, you are better off consulting a financial expert if you are not sure.

- Be sure to consider additional costs. You might incur a lot of hidden charges so be prepared.

Location

The location of your house matters a great deal. It determines much more than what kind of weather you will experience and what kind of neighbors you will have. It will end up affecting your standard of living and quality of life much more than you could ever imagine. Tips for the best location are;

- Look to buy your home in a safe neighborhood. A house should be your sanctuary, so make safety a prime priority before buying a house. Make sure to look at detailed crime statistics of the area before making a purchase. The money you try to save by buying a house in an unsafe neighborhood can cost you your life or that of a loved one. Set your priorities straight and buy a house in a safe location.

- For those who have children, look for areas that have access to top quality schooling. A child's education should not be compromised in any way.

- Look for convenient access to places of entertainment such as malls, cinemas, restaurants, and parks. The more these facilities are nearby, the better the quality of life you will be able to enjoy.

- Selecting a location with a great view makes a home all the more worth living in. Imagine waking to the view of snow-filled mountains or the cool sea breeze blowing through your hair.

- The access to public transit is crucial. Those of you who have jobs that are far away will highly desire easy access to public transit. Apart from that, easy access to public transport makes everything more convenient.

- Easy access to local fire, police and rescue facilities: Be certain to buy a house that has coverage of all these facilities, but never one that is too close. Just imagine living next to a fire station. The noise would make your life miserable.

- Better access to health care is a must when looking for a location to buy a house in. After all, there is no telling when disaster might strike and proximity to a health care facility means the difference between life and death.

Inspection

A proper house inspection will not only make your living easier but also increase the durability of your house and its resale price. Tips on getting the right inspection are;

- Be sure to pick a qualified inspector.

- Have the structural elements inspected? These include the walls, building, and foundations.

- Has the exterior evaluated? This includes paint, landscaping, drainage, and passageways.

- Be sure to have the roof and attic checked. These are usually the problem areas.

- The plumbing should be top on the inspection list. Faulty plumbing is a major loss.

- The heating and cooling systems should be in top working order.

- All the sockets and lighting should be in working condition. The electrical wiring should be in perfect order. You never want faulty wiring to cause major damage.

- If your house has a garage, it should be inspected as it is often ignored in terms of repairs.

Home requirements

An important tip when buying a house is to look for one that fulfills your requirements. Your personal requirements are what make your house your home. They are the individual components that will mold your house according to your individual needs. It is often an ignored fact, but before buying a house, you should always take some time to analyze your current needs and the needs that will arise in the future. This way you could look for a house that will be according to what you desire rather than you having to settle for what you get.

Pre-plan the number of bedrooms that will be needed in the house. If you're expecting more children in the future, then plan accordingly. An extra guest room should be on top of the list for those people that have constant visits from friends and family. It is better to pre-plan, select a house that gives you the bedroom options you desire rather than having to add a bedroom later. That will surely prove to be a rather costly exercise.

A house that is old gives an elegant look and feel. For some people, a traditional-looking house is a factor that is highly desirable. On the other hand, there are those people who have not embraced the new technology and enjoy the modern lifestyle revolution. Try to understand which of these people you are and select your house accordingly. Don't end up buying a thick-walled old house and then wonder why the WIFI signals are so weak.

The bathroom needs are different for different families. If you have more than one child, we suggest you look for a house that has multiple bathrooms. The queue in the morning outside a bathroom could be one of the most annoying feelings in the world. Then there's the little matter of the bathroom design. If you are into the eco-friendly lifestyle, look for houses with plumbing that is efficient before-hand. Changing the whole plumbing could prove to be an expensive exercise.

For some people, outdoor activities are highly desirable. Playing with your pets, catching practice with your kids or just relaxing in the old hammock are all activities that require a decent-sized garden. After buying a house, converting an already built piece of land into a garden will prove to be expensive. Also, the garage space, parking space, and pool requirements should be taken into consideration.

Understanding the monthly costs

The costs of your house are way more than just the price of the property you buy. There are a lot of other costs that need to be understood in order for you to get a true idea of the actual amount of money you will be spending. A lack of knowledge of these costs has led many consumers astray in the past and it is pivotal that you have an understanding of the monthly costs that you will have to incur for years after making that initial purchase.

The mortgage payments, that you have to pay monthly, will have to be looked at carefully. It will depend on the amount of initial principle you pay and the subsequent interest rate the bank sets on them. It is better to consult a financial analyst and get the present value of all future payments calculated so you get an idea of the eventual cost of that house. This will be higher than the principal amount that the real estate agent tells you.

Taxes are something that varies from state to state and region to region. The only taxes you will pay will not be housing tax. As housing tax will be the principle tax you pay, do look into detail on which tax bracket your house will fall into and how much that will cost you. It is imperative that you look into the taxing structure to see if there are any cutbacks that you can avail. Then the local and municipal taxes come into play. Living in very expensive localities will often be paired with paying higher taxes for municipal services. Be sure that those taxes are worth your while.

Insurance costs will end up costing you a lot. First, there is title insurance. Be sure to look at the terms and conditions of the title insurance you purchase so that you don't end up believing that you have something covered when it actually isn't. Housing insurance in your neighborhood should be purchased after conducting a comparative analysis, so you don't pay more than the market average.

Don't forget about the monthly maintenance fee if you are planning to live in a townhouse or a condo. Also, Regular fix-up costs are monthly costs that are often ignored when buying a house. Depending on the condition of the house you're purchasing, the inspection report, the climatic conditions and your neighborhood's proximity to places of public gathering, you will incur regular fix-up costs.

Living in a locality where there is a lot of snowfall or on beach-side with a lot of moisture will cause damage to your house – all the way from your plumbing to your driveway. Living in areas which are close to public places will eventually cost you miscellaneous repairs. If you have damaged or faulty areas in your house, they will also have to be maintained regularly and might cost you a significant chunk of money.

In the end, the monthly costs should be calculated carefully beforehand so that later on you do not feel the sudden financial pressures of these imminent payments.

Picking the right realtor

Choosing the right realtor might mean the difference between buying a house that you will adore Vs one that you may despise. Getting the best deal possible is dependent on getting the realtor that best fits your requirements. The following are some tips to help you find that perfect realtor:

- Meet the agent out in the field and not in their office. This will give you an idea of their quality.

- You must have an agent that has closed a lot of deals. That shows experience. An agent that has experience will never hesitate to knock on doors for you and get you the best deal. He or She will have the know-how and understanding of the market and have more contacts in the field.

- A great tip to meeting agents is to attend open houses. Regardless of the fact that whether you are interested in buying that particular property, attend the open house so that you can meet the best agents there. This will help you further down the road when you want to make your dream purchase.

- Referrals from the people you know and love is a great way to get a good agent. After all the people who care for you will never lead you astray and guide you to an agent that they themselves had an excellent experience with.

- Make sure you get an agent that has moved into the 21st century. Having a tech-savvy agent that is able to text, use email and has a website is crucial to getting the best deal. Most of today's real-estate dealings take place online and on the go. An agent that is not current with the latest trends is sure to lag behind.

- Never settle for an agent at first sight. Do your research. Search and interview as many candidates as possible. This will give you an idea of their quality by comparative analysis. Look at the agreement and read it carefully before signing it. Build trust with the agent- after all, it's your future home which is at stake.

- Look for agents that can give personal time and attention. If an agent is too busy, you might not a good enough deal.

- Look for an agent that has the requisite knowledge. A good salesman with all the sales tips and clichés would be worth nothing if he doesn't have the right knowledge. Ask your agent the things you have learned about. If your agent cannot give you satisfactory answers, move on to another agent.

- A well-respected agent is a must. If he has a good reputation in the market than it is due to hard work and delivering good deals time and time again. Those agents that cannot deliver will not be that well respected in the market.

- Look for agents that live in and near the locality. These agents will then have the right knowledge on all aspects of the area. Agents who are new to the areas of your interest will not be the best option.

- A good agent should go beyond just getting you a house. He should be able to guide you through mortgage brokers, loan officers, financial analysts, and inspectors. All of these references will count in the whole buying process.

- Make sure the agent you hire does this job full time. A part-time agent might have other things on his plate.

- A good agent should have no issues about giving you frequent updates about the transaction

- As you are going to be buying a house, it is best if you work with seasoned buying agents. They will have your interests as a buyer in their minds and help you in the best possible way. Seller's agents will always benefit the seller.

Looking at the resale value

Choosing a home is much more than just a purchase, it is an investment. To make sure you make the right investment, you have to purchase a property with one eye on the resale value. Since buying a home is a substantial purchase, you have to be sure that you don't end up losing money.

There are some key tips on making sure that your home will have a good resale value:

- Be sure to buy in an area which has had constant prices. Neighborhoods that have experienced booms or busts tend to lose your money, but those which have seen their prices remain stable over a number of years tend to be the better option.

- Buy your house in an area that has a low crime rate. Be careful and look at the detailed crime statistics. Keep in mind that the biggest devaluation can often be brought about by high crime rate areas.

- Be sure to have the house inspected for problems and have them fixed before selling so that you can command a higher price.

- Buy homes close to large development projects. This will likely increase the price of land over the next few years and will end up making you a substantial profit.

- Buy a home with more than two bedrooms. This will increase the buyers' market for the house in the future. Many couples need a guest room and an office so more space will tend to sell better.

- A home with more than one bathroom will get you much better resale. A home without a master bath will tend to sell for less.

- Buy a home that has family space. Family space could be anything from a good-sized lounge to a decent sized balcony where people can gather to socialize. This is an attractive resale point.

- A house with good storage space nowadays will get you much better resale. Although we live in a time where less is more, you will be surprised at how much stuff people collect these days. Everything from the size of wardrobes to the storage rooms is increasing. Be mindful of that when purchasing a home.

- A garage is desirable for good resale. Even if you are looking to buy a house that has no garage, having one nonetheless will give you good resale. A garage can be used for multiple purposes and is highly desirable.

- That the layout of the house is structured ergonomically and efficiently is a great advantage to have when reselling the house. Look for the well-designed efficient house as they will never go out of demand.

Clumsily designed houses with an inefficient use of space will always sell for much less.

- Buying a house in a nice neighborhood that has easy access to public transport, leisure, entertainment, schooling, and recreational activities will increase its resale value. Avoid economically depressed neighborhoods where people are not taking care of their houses and there is a lot of clutter on the streets.

CONCLUSION

In order for a piece of real estate to be considered a house, you must feel at home in it. Buying a house is a substantial investment, so it is vital that you think before the purchase and make the purchase decision according to your priorities.

Take care in following the guidelines and tips given in this book, as ultimately they will lead you to buy a home that is more suitable to your needs and that will give you value for your money. Remember that buying the right home will not only guarantee a good return on your investment in terms of resale value, but it will also give you a better future. So buying the house with the right characteristics is the key message of this book.

The homestyle will determine the primary layout of the house and you should keep that in mind whilst making a purchase. Go for the style that best suits your needs. If you don't like stairways, buy a ranch-style house. If you're looking for something elegant and spacious, colonial home is what you'd like. There are many home styles and all have their distinct characteristics so be sure to understand what they represent before making the purchase.

The house should provide a comfortable space for its occupants. There is no universal standard for the amount of square footage that will give you comfortable living space. Be sure to take into consideration the number of people that are going to live and their space needs.

The location of the house is perhaps one of the most important decisions whilst buying a house. The location will not only determine your lifestyle choices, but it will also determine the nearby access to amenities and entertainment. The climate of the locality and conversely your clothing choices all will be determined by location. Be sure to choose a location that is safe from both natural hazards and crime. A house is supposed to be a sanctuary; if you don't feel safe in your own house then that would be a shame.

You have to decide on whether to live in the city amidst the hustle and bustle and pollution or quietly in the countryside. A middle ground is provided by the suburban lifestyle. This decision will impact the property prices, the insurance costs and the cost of living. Everything from transportation, education, and entertainment will be governed by this choice. Be sure to pick wisely.

Whilst looking for houses, stay away from industrial areas and commercial centers. The noise from such areas might affect your sleep patterns. Always try and find a place that is nestled in a well-connected residential area.

Your budget should be the key factor in determining your housing choice. Do not fall into the trap of overspending on your house by taking out large loans or mortgages. If you cannot afford a house try and rent one. The 2007 housing crisis has shown us that the markets are volatile and the bubble can burst. So be cautious of your earning and make your investment wisely.

The housing decision should also revolve around the proximity to your friends and family. Try and incorporate their locations when making a decision. More importantly, remember that there are going to be people living with you. What are their needs, wants, and desires? You have to consider them when making a purchase.

The mortgage rates are often riddled with hidden charges and costs that you might not understand. Before making a mortgage agreement, search the market for comparable deals. Look to get the lowest interest rate but be mindful of rates that seem too good to be true. Scams are also out there so you have to be vigilant and it's best if you contact a financial expert when making this decision.

The costs of rent, mortgage or taxes aren't the only cost of living associated with the house as is popularly believed. You have to be mindful of all the extended cost of living that will be associated with the location you select. The transport cost, the cost of local utilities, the general prices of the local entertainment and leisure activities are also to be looked at. The lifestyle of the neighborhood and how much it will cost you to be part of that will have to be duly calculated.

The local schools and colleges are a very important consideration. If you have young children, then the quality of the public school system should be a top priority. For older children, the quality of colleges and proximity to top colleges is a major plus point.

Personal priorities and choices are not to be ignored. After all, it's your house so it should be according to your taste. It is you who decides on whether to go for a modern or a traditional house. You decide on the floors, bathrooms, kitchen design and design of the interior. Make sure you choose what appeals to you rather than what is suggested by the designers.

The most crucial aspect that this book reiterates is the importance of having a proper inspection. Be sure to choose a certified inspector, be present at the inspection and listen and follow up on the inspection results. Whether you're buying a house that is new or second hand, the importance of a detailed inspection cannot be overstated.

This book will guide you towards making an educated guess and in the end, it is up to you to make the final decision. Choose a home that is according to your needs, the neighborhood that best suits you and the payment method that is easily affordable.

Thank you for reading "The Smart First-Time Home Buyer's Guide". I wish you the best in finding your dream home and have a wonderful first-time homeowner experience.

I just want to thank you one last time for reading" The Smart First-Time home buyer Guide, I hope the information in this book is helpful to you. If you enjoyed this book, please take some time to share your thoughts and post a review.

Thomas.K.Lutz

www.ingramcontent.com/pod-product-compliance
Lightning Source LLC
Chambersburg PA
CBHW060407080526
44583CB00012B/495